Louis Köhler

Practical Method for the Pianoforte

Op. 249

Louis Kohler

Practical Method for the Pianoforte
Op. 249

ISBN/EAN: 9783744781787

Printed in Europe, USA, Canada, Australia, Japan

Cover: Foto ©Thomas Meinert / pixelio.de

More available books at **www.hansebooks.com**

PRACTICAL METHOD

FOR THE
PIANOFORTE

BY

LOUIS KÖHLER

Op. 249

REVISED BY HANS SEMPER

Book I.   (Edition Wood, No. 5)
Book II.   (Edition Wood, No. 6)
Book III. (Edition Wood, No. 7)

The B. F. Wood Music Co.
Boston, New York, Leipzig,
London

Printed in U.S.A.

I. Stroke of the First Finger
Anschlag des ersten Fingers
Attaque du premier doigt

II. Stroke of the Wrist
Anschlag des Handgelenks
Attaque du poignet.

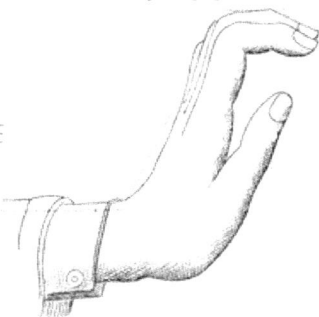

III. Stroke of the Wrist and Forearm combined.
Anschlag des Handgelenks und Unterarms zusammen.
Attaque du poignet et de l'avant bras simultanément.

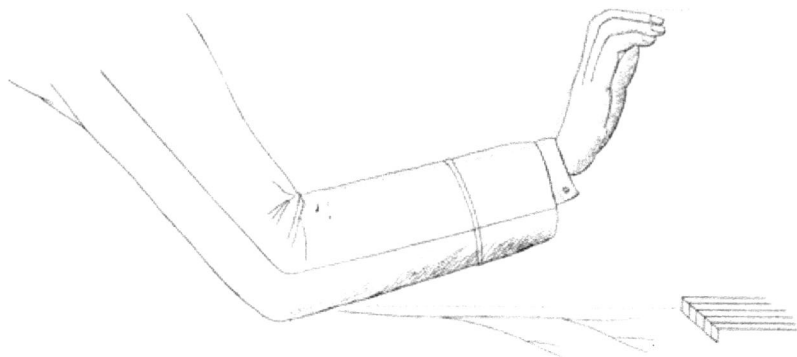

IV. Position of the First Finger for Staccato Stroke.
Stelle des ersten Fingers vor dem Staccato Anschlag
Position du premier doigt pour l'attaque du staccato.

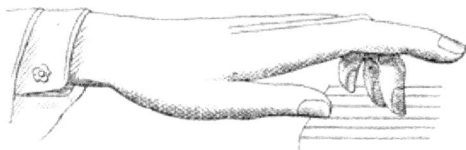

V. Position after the Stroke.
Stelle nach dem Anschlag.
Position après l'attaque

F. W. 4484 · 65

Edition Wood.

Elementary Principles for the Pianist.
Anfangsgründe für die Klavierspieler.
Principes Elémentaires pour le Pianiste.

Staff.	Lines.	Spaces.	Leger Lines.
Notensystem.	*Linien*	*Zwischenräume.*	*Hülfslinien.*
Portée.	Lignes.	Interlignes.	Lignes Supplémentaires.

Treble or G Clef.
Violin oder G Schlüssel.
Clef de Sol.

G
Sol

Bass or F Clef.
Bass oder F Schlüssel.
Clef de Fa.

F
Fa

Notes on the 5 lines.	in the 4 spaces.	above and below the staff.	on the leger lines.
Noten auf den 5 Linien.	*in den 4 Zwischenräumen.*	*ueber und unter dem System.*	*auf den Hülfslinien.*
Notes sur les 5 lignes.	dans les 4 Interlignes.	au-dessus et au-dessous de la portée.	sur les lignes supplémentaires.

E G B(H) D F
Mi Sol Si Ré Fa

F A C E
Fa La Do Mi

G
Sol
D
Ré

C A F
Do La Fa

A C E G
La Do Mi Sol

above the leger lines.
über den Hülfslinien.
au-dessus des lignes supplémentaires.

B(H) G E
Si Sol Mi

Above and below the staff.
Ueber und unter dem System.
Au-dessus et au-dessous de la portée.

B(H) D E A
Si Ré Fa La

under the leger lines.
unter den Hülfslinien.
au-dessous des lignes supplémentaires.

B(H)
Si

E C A F
Mi Do La Fa

D B(H) G
Ré Si Sol

G B(H) D F A
Sol Si Ré Fa La

A C E G
La Do Mi Sol

F
Fa

C E G
Do Mi Sol

D F A
Ré Fa La

To facilitate the learning of the notes the pupil must learn well the musical alphabet: c d e f g a b in succession as well as in thirds: ce gb df ac, backward and forward, and must apply this to the notes and keys.

Zur leichten Erlernung der Noten muss der Schüler das musikalische Alphabet: c d e f g a h, nach Terzenschritten: ce gb df ac, vorwärts und rückwärts geläufig hersagen lernen und dies auf die Tasten und Noten anwenden.

Pour faciliter l'étude des notes l'élève doit bien apprendre l'alphabet musical: do, re, mi, fa, sol, la, si, dans leur ordre naturel aussi bien qu'en tierces: do-mi, sol-si, ré-fa, la-do, tant en montant qu'en descendant, et doit s'appliquer aux notes et au clavier.

Intervals. — Intervalle. — Intervalles.

Second	Third	Fourth	Fifth	Sixth	Seventh	Octave
Sekunde	*Terz*	*Quarte*	*Quinte*	*Sexte*	*Septime*	*Oktave*
Seconde	Tierce	Quarte	Quinte	Sixte	Septième	Octave

Edition Wood.

Names of the notes with sharps.(♯)
Namen der Noten mit Kreuzen.(♯)
Noms des Notes avec dièses(♯)

Names of the notes with flats.(♭)
Namen der Noten mit Been.(♭)
Noms des Notes avec bémols.(♭)

C♯	D♯	E♯	F♯	G♯	A♯	B♯	C♯	C♭	D♭	E♭	F♭	G♭	A♭	B♭	C♭
Cis	*Dis*	*Eis*	*Fis*	*Gis*	*Ais*	*His*	*Cis*	*Ces*	*Des*	*Es*	*Fes*	*Ges*	*As*	*B*	*Ces*
Do♯	Ré♯	Mi♯	Fa♯	Sol♯	La♯	Si♯	Do♯	Do♭	Ré♭	Mi♭	Fa♭	Sol♭	La♭	Si♭	Do♭

Chromatic.
Chromatisch.
Cromatique.

C	C♯	D	D♯	E	F	F♯	G	G♯	A	A♯	B	C	B	B♭	A	A♭	G	G♭	F	E	E♭	D	D♭	C
C	*Cis*	*D*	*Dis*	*E*	*F*	*Fis*	*G*	*Gis*	*A*	*Ais*	*H*	*C*	*H*	*B*	*A*	*As*	*G*	*Ges*	*F*	*E*	*Es*	*D*	*Des*	*C*
Do	D♯	Re	Re♯	Mi	Fa	Fa♯	Sol	Sol♯	La	La♯	Si	Do	Si	Si♭	La	La♭	Sol	Sol♭	Fa	Mi	Mi♭	Ré	Ré♭	Do

Enharmonic.
Enharmonisch.
Enharmonique.

		Black keys.								
		Schwarze Tasten.								
		Touches noires.								

White keys.	C	D	E F♭	F E♯	G	A	B C♭	C B♯
Weisse Tasten.	*C*	*D*	*E Fes*	*F Eis*	*G*	*A*	*H Ces*	*C His*
Touches blanches.	Do	Ré	Mi Fa♭	Fa Mi♯	Sol	La	Si Do♭	Do Si♯

Keyboard of Seven Octaves.

Clavier de Sept Octaves.

Abbildung einer Klaviatur von Sieben Octaven.

Treble Clef.
Violin Schlüssel.
Clef de Sol.

Bass Clef.
Bass Schlüssel.
Clef de Fa.

Value and Form of the Notes and Rests. — Werth und Gestalt der Noten und Pausen.
Valeur et Forme des Notes et Silences.

Notes. — *Noten.* — Notes.

Rests.
Pausen oder Schweigezeichen.
Silences.

Whole Note. *Ganze Note.* Ronde.	Whole Rest. *Ganze Pause.* Pause.
Half Notes. *Halbe Noten.* Blanches.	Half Rests. *Halbe Pausen.* Demi-pauses.
4 Quarter Notes. *4 Viertel Noten.* 4 Noires.	Quarter Rests. *Viertel Pausen.* Soupirs.
8 Eighth Notes. *8 Achtel Noten.* 8 Croches.	Rests. *Pausen.* Soupirs.
4 Triplets. *4 Triolen.* 4 Triolets.	
16 Sixteenth Notes. *16 Sechszehntel Noten.* 16 Double Croches.	
32 Thirty-second Notes. *32 Zweiunddreissigstel Noten.* 32 Triple Croches.	
64 Sixty-fourth Notes. *64 Vierundsechszigstel Noten.* 64 Quadruple Croches.	

Dot after a note.
Punkt hinter einer Note.
Point après une note.

Two dots after a note.
Zwei Punkte hinter einer Note.
Deux points après une note.

etc.

Value. – *Werth.* – Valeur.

Dot after a rest.
Punkt hinter einer Pause.
Point après un silence.

Two dots after a rest.
Zwei Punkte hinter einer Pause.
Deux points après un silence.

etc.

Value – *Werth* – Valeur.

Bars (or Measures.)
Takte. Mesures.

Brace. Klammer. Parenthèse.

Barlines.
Taktstriche.
Barres de mesure.

The various divisions of time used in Music are as follows:
Die in der Musik vorkommenden Taktarten sind:
Les differentes divisions du temps employées en musique sont les suivantes:

Common Time. *Vier Viertel Takt.* Quatre Temps.	Triple Time. *Drei Viertel Takt.* Trois Temps.	Half Common Time. *Zwei Viertel Takt.* Deux Temps.	Triple Time. *Drei Achtel Takt.* Mesure à trois huit.
Compound Common Time. *Sechs Achtel Takt.* Six huit.	Compound Triple Time. *Neun Achtel Takt.* Neuf huit.	Twelve Eight Time. *Zwölf Achtel Takt.* Douze huit.	Duple Time. (Alla breve). *Zwei Halbe Takt, (Alla breve).* C barre.

Accidentals. — Versetzungszeichen. — Alterations.

Sharp. *Kreuz.* Dièse.	Flat. *Be.* Bèmol.	Natural. *Auflösungszeichen.* Bécarre.					
			C. C sharp. C natural.		D. D flat. D natural.		
			C. Cis. C.		*D. Des. D.*		
			Do. Do dièse. Do bécarre.		Ré. Ré bemol. Ré bécarre.		

B.F.W. 4556-55

Edition Wood

4

FIRST EXERCISES
for the hand of rest.

DIE ERSTEN ÜBUNGEN
mit stillstehender Hand.

EXERCICES
à main posée.

The fingering above the notes is intended for the right hand, that below for the left, which is to play the notes one or two octaves lower than written.-

Repeat each passage from 10 to 20 times.

Die obern Ziffern gelten für die rechte, die untern für die linke Hand, welche eine Octave oder deren zwei tiefer spielt –

Jeder Teil ist 10 bis 20 Mal nacheinander zu spielen.

Le doigté supérieur s'applique à la main droite, le doigté inférieur à la main gauche, qui doit jouer une ou deux octaves plus bas.-

Répéter 10 fois 20 fois chaque reprise.

Repeat these exercises with both hands, and continue their practice while studying the following pieces

Nun sind diese Übungen auch zweibändig zu spielen und während der folgenden Stücke zu wiederholen.

Répéter ces exercices à deux mains et les jouer fréquemment dans l'intervalle des pieces qui suivent.

Edition Wood

6

STACCATO EXERCISES.

In the following exercises the stroke is not made with the finger, but from the wrist, the finger which touches the keys being held slightly lower than the others.

Repeat each passage 6 times.

STACCATO-ÜBUNG.

Bei den folgenden Übungen ist der Anschlagfinger nicht zu bewegen, während er fest im Gelenke bleibt, wird die ganze Hand durch das Handgelenk auf und ab bewegt.

Jeder Teil 6 Mal

EXERCICES DE STACCATO.

Les exercices qui suivent doivent être joués par l'articulation du poignet, le doigt restant immobile.

Répéter 6 fois chaque reprise.

Child's Song.   Kinder-Liedchen.   Mélodie Enfantine.

Melodie.

FINGER EXERCISES.
Repeat each exercise 8 times.

FINGER ÜBUNGEN.
Jeder Teil 8 Mal.

EXERCICES
Répéter 8 fois chaque reprise.

Practice these exercises with the hands singly and together, and in alternation with the pieces which follow.

Diese Übungen sind ein- und zweihändig zu spielen und während der folgenden Stücke fortzusetzen.

Ces exercices doivent être joués à une et à deux mains, et repétés dans l'intervalle des pieces qui suivent.

Edition Wood.

22.

23.

Children's Waltz.   Kinder - Walzer.   Valse d'Enfants.

Allegretto moderato.

24.

Edition Wood.

FINGER EXERCISES.
Repeat each exercise 8 times

FINGER-ÜBUNGEN.
Jeder Teil 8 mal.

EXERCICES.
Repeter 8 fois chaque reprise

Allegretto.

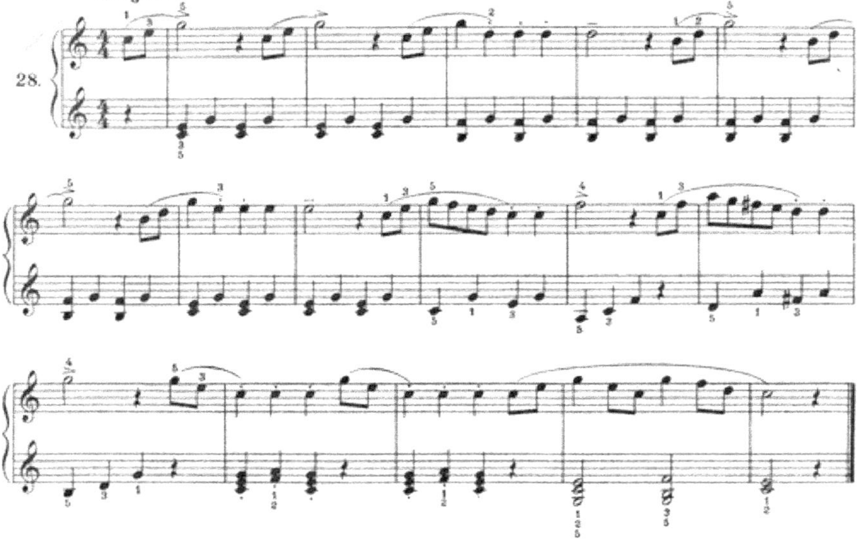

Allegretto.

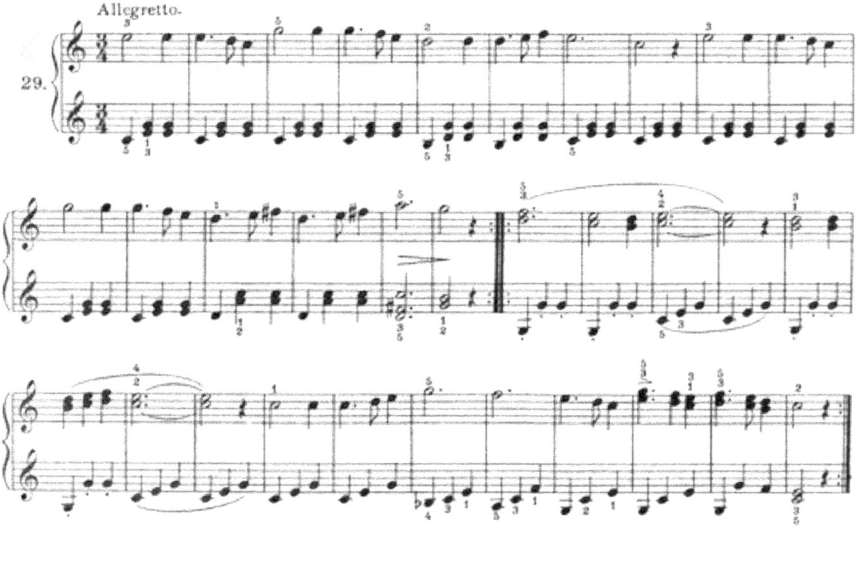

EXERCISES
for the hand at rest

UBUNGEN
mit stillstehender Hand

EXERCICES
à main posée.

To make all the fingers of both hands of equal strength and independence the following exercise must be practiced with each hand alone and then with both hands together, until they can be played without constraint and with proper fluency. Take particular care that the hands are held quietly, and that the fingers are raised lightly and do not remain longer on the keys than is necessary.

Um allen Fingern beider Hände gleiche Kraft und Unabhängigkeit zu verschaffen, müssen diese Übungen anfangs mit jeder Hand einzeln, dann mit beiden zusammen so lange geübt werden, bis sie ohne Zwang und mit gehöriger Rundung vorgetragen werden. Besonders erinnere man sich dabei der Regel, die Hände ganz ruhig zu halten, die Finger leicht fortzubewegen und sie nicht länger auf den Tasten liegen zu lassen, als es nötig ist.

Pour donner à tous les doigts des deux mains une même force et de l'indépendance, il faut d'abord jouer ces exercices d'une seule main, puis des deux ensemble jusqu'à ce qu'ils soient joués sans raideur. Que l'on ait soin surtout de tenir les mains bien tranquilles, de lever les doigts légèrement, et de ne pas les laisser sur les touches plus longtemps qu'il n'est nécessaire.

In the Garden.   Im Garten.   Au Jardin.

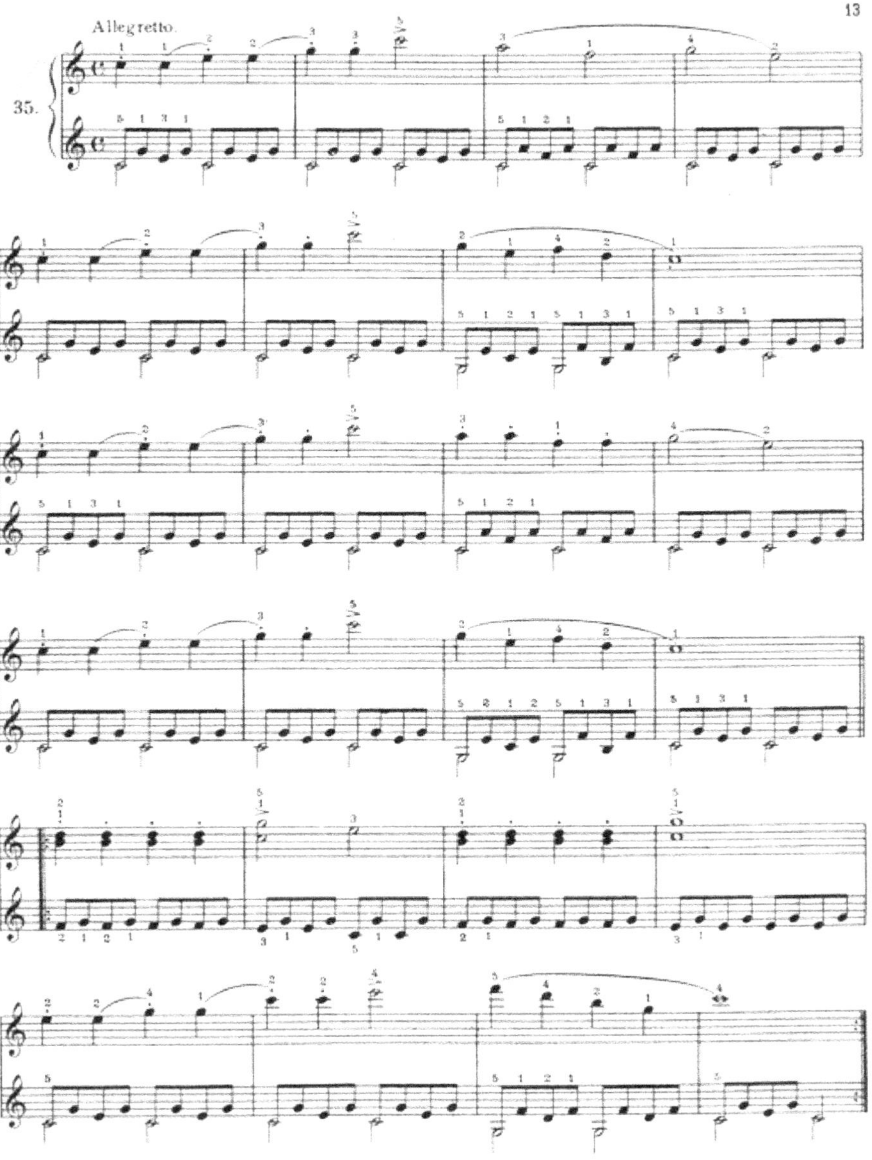
Allegretto.
35.

EXERCISES.
Repeat each passage 20 times.

ÜBUNGEN.
Jeder Teil 20 Mal

EXERCICES.
Répéter 20 fois chaque reprise.

39.

Allegretto.

EXERCISE
for the hand at rest.

ETUDE
mit stillstehender Hand.

EXERCICE
à main posée.

40.

Edition Wood.

About the Lamb.
Folk-song.

Vom Schäfchen.
Volkslied.

De l'Agneau.
Air populaire.

Andantino.

41.

FINGER EXERCISES
on the bass notes.

The left hand plays the notes as written, the right hand one or two octaves
higher.

FINGER-ÜBUNGEN
in Bassnoten.

Die Linke spielt die folgenden Bassnoten wie sie dastehen, die Rechte eine
Octave oder deren zwei höher

EXERCICES
en clef de fa.

La main gauche doit jouer ces notes
comme elles sont écrites, la main droite
une octave ou deux plus haut.

42.

LITTLE PIECES
with bass notes.

KLEINE STÜCKE
mit Bassnoten.

PETITS MORCEAUX
en clef de fa.

A. E. MULLER.

43.

44.

Edition Wood.

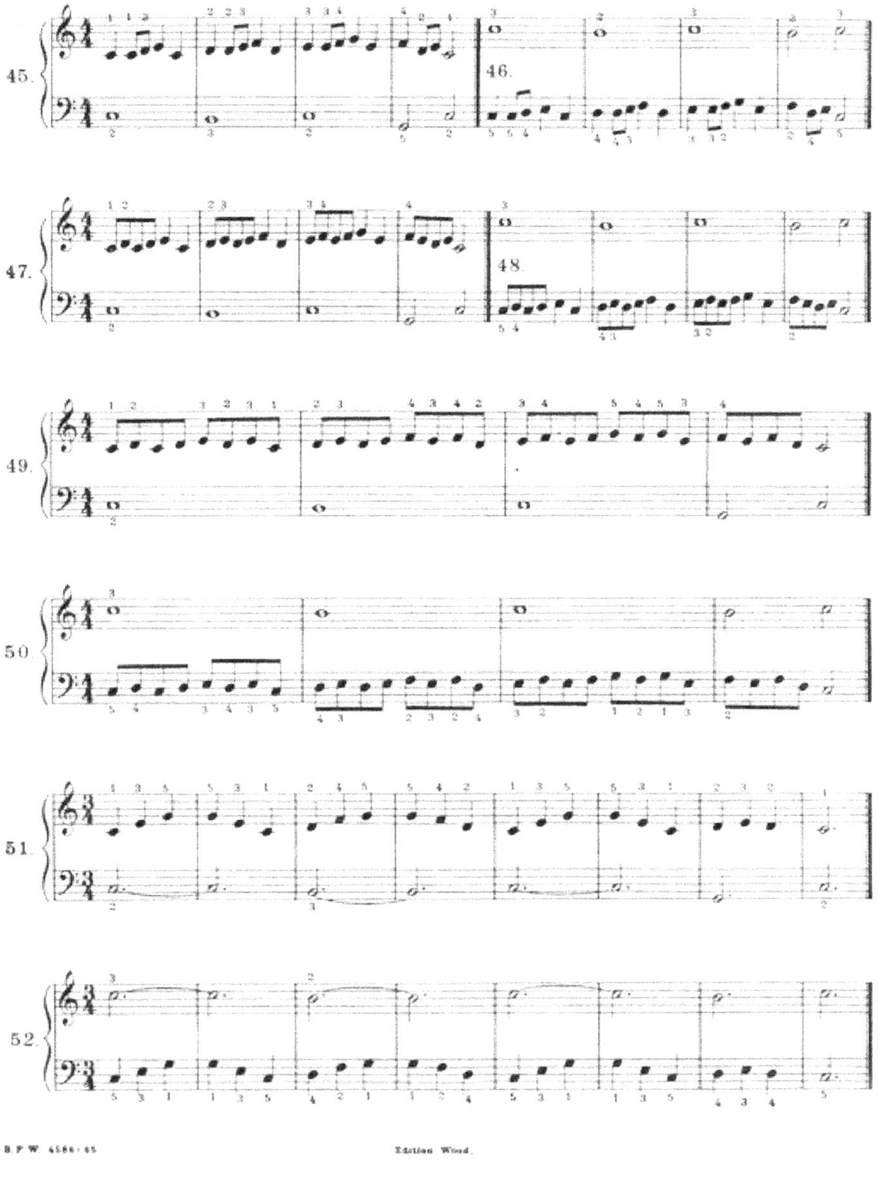
45.
46.
47.
48.
49.
50.
51.
52.

Edition Wood.

The Cuckoo.
Folk-Song.

Kuckuck.
Volkslied.

Le Coucou.
Air Populaire.

Allegretto moderato.

58.

ADVANCING THE HAND
by repetition of the fingering.

FORTBEWEGEN DER HÄNDE
durch Anziehen der Finger.

ETUDES
de Progressions.

59.

Edition Wood.

Melodie.

60.

Etude.

61.

Lied.

62.

Choral.

63.

Folk-song.   Volkslied.   Air Populaire.

64. Andantino.

Etude.

*) Notes, which, if played at the sametime, form an harmonic chord, are frequently played "legatissimo." This is accomplished by allowing the fingers to remain on their respective keys. (See example).

*) Accordische Figuren (d. i. nacheinanderfolgende Töne, welche zusammen angeschlagen einen harmonischen Accord bilden) werden öfters "legatissimo" gespielt, dies geschieht, indem man die Töne eines Accordes dauernd festhält, hier z. B. so:

*) Des notes qui, frappées à la fois, forment un accord harmonique, se jouent fréquemment "legatissimo." Dans ce cas, les doigts doivent rester appliqués aux touches respectives.

Allegretto con Variazioni.

A. E. MÜLLER.

VAR. 1.

VAR. 2.

Edition Wood

VAR. 3.

VAR. 4.

Ring dance   Reigen im Spiel.   Récréation.

Song of the Hussars.   Husarenlied.   Chant de Hussards.

69.

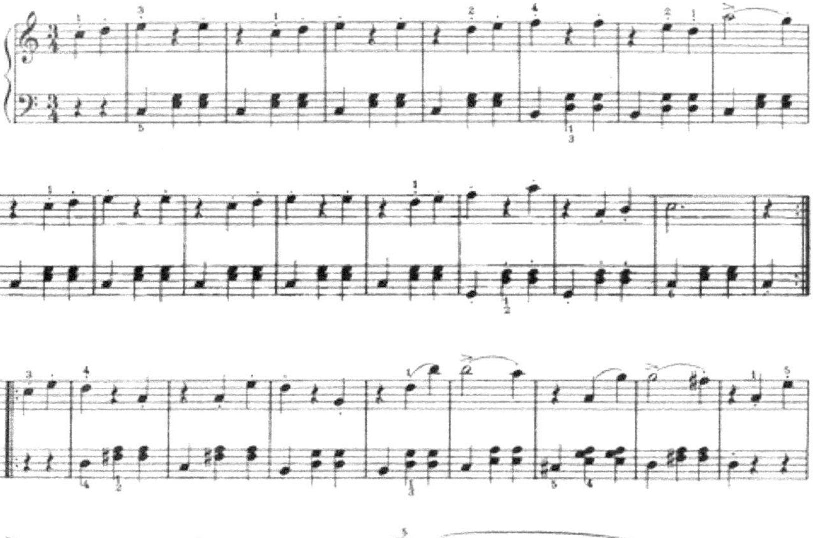

EXERCISES
on the higher bass notes.

ÜBUNGEN
in höheren Bassnoten.

EXERCICES
en clef de fa.

70.

THEME
with variations.

THEMA
mit Variationen.

THEME
avec variations.

THEMA.   VAR. 1.   J. N. HUMMEL.

71.

VAR. 2.   VAR. 3.

VAR. 4.   VAR. 5.

VAR. 6.

VAR. 7.

VAR. 8.

VAR. 9.

VAR. 10.

Evening Song.   Abendlied.   Chant du Soir.

Andantino.

72.

Edition Wood

Gieb mir die Blume, gieb mir den Kranz.

German melody.   Deutsches Lied   Air Allemand.

30

Moderato.

J. WANHALL.

75.

mf

EXERCISES
for the passing of the thumb.

ERSTE ÜBUNGEN
im Unter- und Übersetzen.

EXERCICES
pour le passage du pouce.

Right hand. — *Rechts.* — Main droite.

76.

Left hand. — *Links* — Main gauche

77.

Right hand. — *Rechts.* — Main droite.

78.

Left hand. — *Links.* — Main gauche.

79.

Etude.

Allegretto.

80.

*) Formulas for Scale practice, which should be begun here, may be found on pages 62, 63 and 64.

*) Formeln zur Tonleiterubung, die hier anfangen sollte, erscheinen auf Seiten 62, 63 und 64.

*) Les formules pour l'étude des gammes, qui peut être commencée ici, seront trouvées aux pages 62, 63 et 64.

B.F.W. 4566-65

Edition Wood.

Villager's Waltz.   Ländlicher Walzer.   Valse Villageoise.

Choral.

Française.

Etude.

Edition Wood.

Air
from the Magic Flute.

Lied
aus der Zauberflöte.

Air
de la Flûte enchantée.

W. A. MOZART

Andantino.

85.

mf

legato

rit.

a tempo

f

Edition Wood

34

The Brook.   Der Bach fliesst.   Le Ruisseau.

86.

Contentment.   Zufriedenheit.   Contentement.
Folk-song.   Volkslied.   Air populaire.

87.

Etude.

88.

Edition Wood.

36

Melody from
"Der Freischütz."

Melodie aus
"Der Freischütz."

Mélodie tirée du
"Der Freischütz."

C. M. v WEBER.

89.

Etude.

90.

Edition Wood

Etude.

91.

Fidolin.

Italian Folk-song   Italienisches Volkslied   Air populaire Italien

92.

Allegretto.

93.

Viennese Couplet.   Wiener Couplet.   Couplet Viennois.

Moderato.

94.

Etude.

95.

Russian Folk-song.   Russisches Volkslied.   Air Populaire Russe.

Duettino from "Titus."   Duettino aus "Titus."   Duettino de "Titus."

W. A. MOZART

Etude.

Andantino.
J. WANHALL
99.
f
Execution
Ausführung
Execution
Allegretto.
J. WANHALL
100.
mf
f
p
f
ritard.
mf a tempo
f

Etude.

Christmas Bells.   Weihnachtsglocken.   Les Cloches de Noël.

Edition Wood.

Allegretto con Variazioni.

A. F. MÜLLER

103.

VAR. I

43

VAR. 2.
dolce ed un poco vivace
Fine
D.C.
VAR. 3.
staccato
mf
legato
Fine
D.C.
VAR. 4.
Vivace.
f
Fine
D.C.

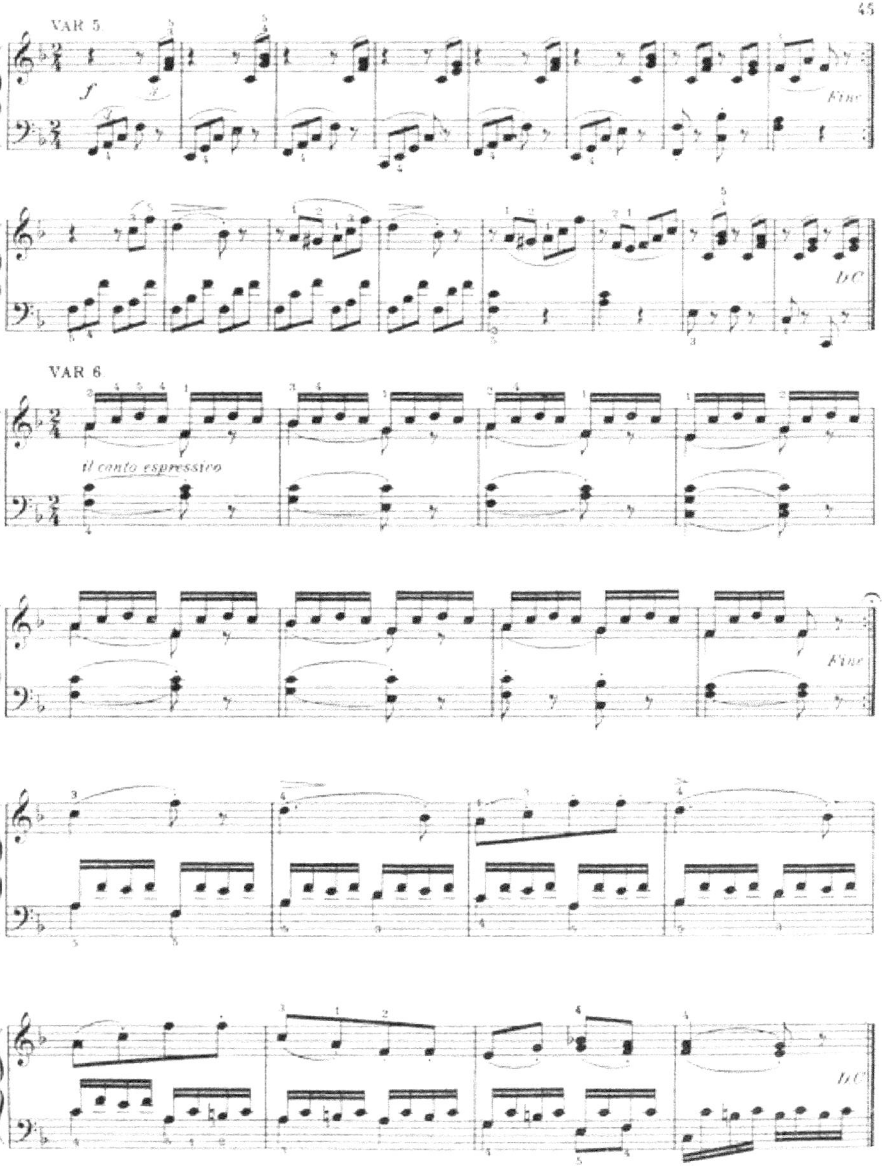
VAR 5.
f
Fine
D.C.
VAR 6.
il canto espressivo
Fine
D.C.

46

Minuet from "Don Juan". | Menuett aus „Don Juan." | Menuet de "Don Juan."

104.

The Murmuring Spring. | Die Quelle Murmelt. | La Source Murmure.

105.

Etude.

Romance from "Joseph".   Romanze aus "Joseph".   Romance de "Joseph".

F. MÉHUL.

Andante

sempre legato

107.

FURTHER EXERCISES
for the passing of the thumb.

WEITERE ÜBUNGEN
im Unter- und Übersetzen.

EXERCICES
pour le passage du pouce.

Right hand — *Rechte Hand.* — Main droite.

108.

SCALE OF C MAJOR.
Repeat 6 times

C DUR-TONLEITER.
Jeder Teil 6 mal

GAMME D'UT MAJEUR.
Repeter 6 fois chaque reprise.

SCALES AND STACCATO.　　TONLEITER UND STACCATO.　　GAMMES ET STACCATO.

Allegro vivo.

C. CZERNY.

113.

Allegretto.

114.

Allegro.

SCALES.
Repeat 10 times.

TONLEITER-LÄUFE.
Jeder Teil 10 mal.

GAMMES.
Répéter 10 fois chaque reprise.

Right hand — Rechts — Main droite

115.

Left hand — Links — Main gauche

116.

Edition Wood.

Right hand — *Rechts* — Main droite

117.

Left hand — *Links* — Main gauche

118.

Allegro.

119.

52

La Guaracha.

Spanish Dance.   Spanischer Tanz.   Danse Espagnole.

Allegro moderato.

120.

Etude.

121.

B. F. W. 4598-65   Edition Wood.

Child's Morning Prayer.   Kindes Morgengebet.   Prière du Matin de l'Enfant.

Andantino

122

54   Children's Waltz.   Kinder Walzer.   Valse d'Enfants.

EXERCISES FOR ONE HAND.   EINHÄNDIGE PASSAGEN-ÜBUNGEN.   EXERCICES POUR UNE MAIN.

Repeat each exercise 12 times.   Jeder Teil 12 mal.   Répéter 12 fois chaque reprise.

Etude.

A. E. MULLER

128.

129. Andante.

130. A. E. MULLER

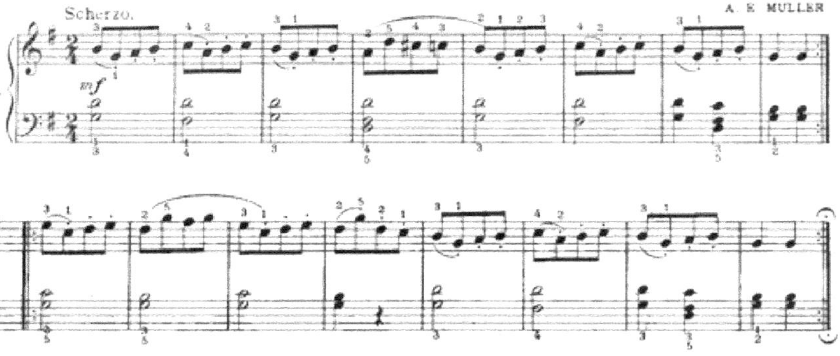

131. A. E. MÜLLER.

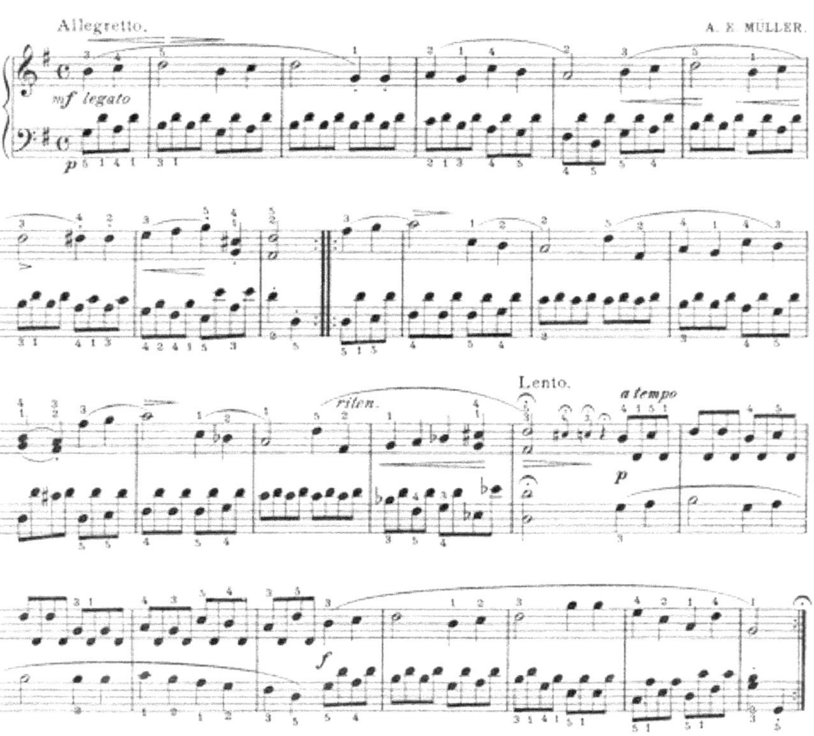

Etude.

C. CZERNY

132.

*) See foot note page 64
*) Siehe Anmerkung auf S. 64
*) Voyez note au bas de la page 64

B F W 4586-44

Edition Wood.

Tyrolese Waltz   Tyroler Walzer.   Valse Tyrolienne.

133.

Etude.

134

Choral.

135.

Polish Melody.   Polnisches Lied.   Air Polonais.

136.

EXERCISE IN WRIST MOVEMENT. | **ÜBUNG IM HANDGELENK-ANSCHLAG.** | **EXERCICE DU POIGNET.**
Repeat each passage 4 times. | Jeder Teil 4 mal. | Répéter 4 fois chaque reprise.

137.

Edition Wood.

At the Children's Ball. | Auf dem Kinderball. | Le Bal d'Enfants.

Allegretto moderato.

138.

VARIATIONS
on a German Song.

VARIATIONEN
über: Kommt ein Vogel geflogen.

VARIATIONS
sur un Thème Allemand.

HENRY COLMAR.

Moderato.

139.

Kommt ein Vogel ge-flogen, setzt sich nieder auf mein' Fuss, hat ein'n Zettel im Schnabel und vom Dirnel ein' Gruss.

VAR.1.

VAR.2.

B. F. W. 4384-64.   Edition Wood.

The Major Scales, with Fingering.   Die Dur-Tonleiter, mit Fingersatz.
Les Gammes Majeures, avec Doigté.

C major.— *C dur.*— Do majeur.

G major.— *G dur.*—Sol majeur

F major.— *F dur.* - Fa majeur.

D major.— *D dur.* —Ré majeur.

B flat major.— *B dur.*—Si♭ majeur.

A major.— *A dur* —La majeur.

E flat major.— *Es dur.*—Mi♭ majeur.

E major.— *E dur.*—Mi majeur.

A flat major.— *As dur.*—La♭ majeur

B major.— *B dur.*— Si majeur.

D flat major.— *Des dur.*—Ré♭ majeur.

F sharp major. —*Fis dur* —Fa♯ majeur.

G flat major.— *Ges dur.*—Sol♭ majeur.

B.V.W. 6588-15

Edition Wood.

Formula for Scale Practice. | Formeln zur Tonleiterübung.
Formules pour l'Etude des Gammes.

Similar motion. — *Gleichlaufende-bewegung* — Mouvement direct.
N°1. *Both hands legato.* — *Beide Hände legato.* — *Les deux mains legato.*

Contrary motion. — *Gegenbewegung.* — Mouvement contraire.
N°2. *Both hands legato* — *Beide Hände legato.* — *Les deux mains legato.*

Practice Formulas 3, 4, 5 and 6 also in contrary motion.
Man übe Formeln 3, 4, 5 und 6 auch in Gegenbewegung.
Etudiez les Formules 3, 4, 5 et 6 aussi en mouvement contraire.

N°3. *R.H. m.d. staccato, L.H. m.g. legato.*

N°4. *R.H. m.d. legato, L.H. m.g. staccato.*

N°5. *R.H. m.d. slurred, L.H. m.g. legato.*

N°6. *R.H. m.d. legato, L.H. m.g. slurred.*

Practise also both hands slurred, and both hands *staccato*, in similar and in contrary motion.	Man übe auch beide Hände gebunden, und beide Hände *staccato*, in Gleichlaufende-und Gegenbewegung.	Etudiez aussi avec les deux mains en passages liés et *staccato*, en mouvement direct et contraire.

Formula for Scale Practice. (Continued) | Formeln zur Tonleiterübung. (Fortsetzung)
Formules pour l'Etude des Gammes. (Suite)

B I W 4 I46 65
W. Z.

Edition Wood.

At the Circus.
EIGHT SILHOUETTES.
By J. Henry Francis, Op. 27.

The above complete in one Volume (Edition Wood No. 832) Price 75 Cents. 1/6 Net.
Entire List Copyright.

THE B.F. WOOD MUSIC CO.
BOSTON, NEW YORK, LONDON, LEIPZIG.

www.ingramcontent.com/pod-product-compliance
Lightning Source LLC
Chambersburg PA
CBHW021513090426
42739CB00007B/592